ON A 2 MISSION TRANSITION

ON A 2 MISSION TRANSITION

JENNIFER ROBINSON-NEWTON

XULON PRESS

Xulon Press
555 Winderley Pl, Suite 225
Maitland, FL 32751
407.339.4217
www.xulonpress.com

xulon
PRESS

© 2024 by JENNIFER ROBINSON-NEWTON

All rights reserved solely by the author. The author guarantees all contents are original and do not infringe upon the legal rights of any other person or work. No part of this book may be reproduced in any form without the permission of the author.

Due to the changing nature of the Internet, if there are any web addresses, links, or URLs included in this manuscript, these may have been altered and may no longer be accessible. The views and opinions shared in this book belong solely to the author and do not necessarily reflect those of the publisher. The publisher therefore disclaims responsibility for the views or opinions expressed within the work.

Unless otherwise indicated, Scripture quotations taken from the English Standard Version (ESV). Copyright © 2001 by Crossway, a publishing ministry of Good News Publishers. Used by permission. All rights reserved. Scripture quotations taken from the Holy Bible, New International Version (NIV). Copyright © 1973, 1978, 1984, 2011 by Biblica, Inc.™. Used by permission. All rights reserved. Scripture quotations taken from the New King James Version (NKJV). Copyright © 1982 by Thomas Nelson, Inc. Used by permission. All rights reserved. Scripture quotations taken from the King James Version (KJV)–*public domain.*

Paperback ISBN-13: 979-8-86850-424-2
Ebook ISBN-13: 979-8-86850-425-9

DEDICATION

"To my Heavenly Father and my Lord and Savior and the Holy Spirit, who never stopped believing in me."

"For my Heavenly Father who's shown me blessings with whatever is needed for his perfect will to be accomplished."

"To my Lord and Savior, who continues to give me Love, Truth, Unity, Peace and Freedom."

"To the Holy Spirit, who sanctifies me, helps me and leads me to the Father and Son."

"Thank you God for instilling the knowledge and reminding me through the Holy Spirit that Your power can change lives."

ON A MISSION 2 TRANSITION

Jennifer Robinson - Newton

CHAPTER 1

I was born in Bastrop Louisiana on November 5th 1979. I was raised in the state of Arkansas while both of my parents attended universities up until the age of four.

We traveled as a family back and forth until they decided for us to become fully stable in our hometown Bastrop. At the age of four, I attended Northside Elementary my kindergarten school year. I can't recall coming across too many things at this age to leave a mark but I do recall a shift taking place once I attended my second grade school year.

At this stage in my life, I began to notice particular classmates being extremely rude and envious over the pettiest things you could ever imagine. You wouldn't even think that kids at this particular age would have so much envy and hatred in their hearts.

I was too terrified to speak up and defend myself because I was surrounded by an environment that I didn't know existed and having that mentality, things turned for the worse.

The bullying was due to my mother dressing me quite well on a regular basis along with having long black silky hair down my back and some of them envied that. One day while playing on the monkey bars my classmates, Iesha and Terreka, decided they were going to jump me for no apparent reason. As I was being jumped I heard this voice saying, "Stop!". I looked over and it was Neisha from the other classroom.

Neisha was completely dumbfounded! She grabbed me by the hand and said "Let me walk you in the building". As we were walking up the hill, we bumped into one of the teachers and she asked us what happened and once we explained everything she told me to go and report it to my teacher.

When we made it to the classroom I told my teacher, Mrs. Hill, what happened to me and she just simply said go and wash your face and she proceeded to do what she was doing. Back in the day action wasn't taken that seriously. Students pretty much got away with murder. My third grade year I remember climbing up the seesaw and my classmate Marcus lifted the bottom of the seesaw and I fell over and hit my head on the rail and hit the ground. Once I hit the ground all I could hear was laughter and this time around there was no one to pick me up off the ground.

This type of behavior towards me went on every school year. It got to the point of me accepting the bullying because I had become accustomed to it.

My 6th grade year was pretty disturbing. At this time I didn't realize how many students my age were having sexual encounters and that puzzled me because I was still playing with dolls. One day in class, one of my classmates. Marquise asked me to be his girlfriend and out of fear I said, "Yes".

The day after we became a couple he wrote me a letter asking me to indulge in explicit activities with him but I never responded. I ended up misplacing the letter and it ended up getting into the hands of another classmate.

Even though I was being pressured to engage into those sexual activities, I was too terrified to even go pass kissing a boy. Weeks later after his proposal, he tried to hook me up with his buddy, Mickey. Marquise walked me over to Mickey and he said, "Jennifer wants to be your girlfriend" and I said "No I do not.". As I continued to say no, Marquise popped me in the face with a rubber band until I agreed with him.

I felt embarrassed about what I was allowing people to do to me. Getting abused by classmates became normal for me and I just chose to accept it. It felt as if I had this negative and demonic attachment because most encounters, I was being either bullied or humiliated in some type of way.

When I started attending middle school, I tried to fit into certain crowds. I was tired of being an outcast to people. I felt as if it was something I needed to prove. I wanted to be accepted. I'd sit back and observe the toughest girls in class and after observing them I'd ease my way into having a conversation with them.

Once they accepted me, they used me to run their errands around the school or whatever else that benefited them. It was a relief to hang with girls that bully other classmates. After a short while of pretending, I left the group and started concentrating on what really matters in life.

My 8th grade school year, I started stepping out a little bit more. I tried out for basketball and surprisingly I made the team. Our first practice, certain girls on the team weren't too fond of me and began to pick with me. I was like here we go again with the bullying. Enduring that, I began to lose more confidence in myself and instead of pushing myself harder, I fell into that same trap that continued to haunt me everyday of my life.

I couldn't express my true talent because I kept allowing fear and what people thought of me to control me. Proper training outside of the school would've helped, however, my father, who was a basketball coach, helped the best way he could but it was only a certain amount of time that we spent together due to my parents being divorced.

One day during practice, I went in for a layup and missed. My teammate Latesha jumped down my throat about it and as she continued to yell I walked off and went to report it to Coach Burner. When the Coach was around, they didn't say or do too much to me but as soon as she'd step away they'd have their way with me.

I went to Coach Burner in tears and I said I can't take this anymore and they will not leave me alone and they're always rude and beating up on me. She asked, "Who's picking on you?". I didn't want to name any names because I didn't want to be labeled as a snitch.

She looked at me and said I will call everyone in here right now. I was exiting the room and told her that I'm quitting the team. It was not just the girls that upset me but it was a build up from everything that happened to me over the years and that was my breaking point.

ON A MISSION 2 TRANSITION

Chapter 1

FEAR
Isaiah 41:10

Fear not, I am with you; be not dismayed, for I am your God; I will strengthen you: I will help you, I will uphold you with my righteous hand

CHAPTER 2

When my mother left the state of Louisiana, it hurt me to my soul. It was the first time in my life experiencing what true pain feels like. It felt like a piece of me was gone. I'm sure it was the same for my sister.

My mother and I left each other not being on the best of terms and it was an open wound that continued to linger. Enduring that, my spirit began to attract more attention to the wrong type of people, due to the abandonment feeling I had.

My mother didn't abandon us with true intentions but I feel she was hurt behind us playing a part in telling family members what was going on inside our home.

It was selfish on our end in some ways to judge her life but we were so used to things being a certain way for so many years.

Shortly after my mom left us, I started dating this guy, Frederick. I met him in high school. When we'd see each other in the hallway he'd always say "Will you be my girlfriend?".

I would brush him off because he was a junior and I was a senior. He asked me to go to prom with him but I declined. A year later, our paths crossed again at our hometown carnival.

He was walking with a group of friends and he saw me and said "Jennifer!". I walked over to him and he said, "Girl, you are still looking good!". We walked and talked and ended up spending the rest of the night together.

Leaving the carnival, Frederick decided to drive me home. On the way home, we pulled up to a park. I started to think, "Why are we at a park at this time of night?". We got out and he grabbed my hand and we went for a walk in the park. On our way to the bench, he grabbed me from behind. I knew exactly what he was trying to do.

Once he got me to the bench he kissed me but I couldn't surrender because I was saving myself until marriage. He whispered, "I will not hurt you." I responded, "I can't because I'm a virgin." He responded saying well you didn't kiss him like a virgin. I decided it was pretty late and he continued trying to get me there but I pulled away while grabbing his hands to lead me to his car.

The next day he called to see how I was doing and asked if he could come over to spend some time with me. I allowed him to come over and it seemed like within seconds his car door slammed. I was so nervous. He knocked on the door and it took me back to Betty Wright's hit song "Tonight is the Night".

I opened the door and before I could say anything, one thing led to another. I felt horrible and guilty! I didn't judge him because both of us played a part in sin.

Once he got me where he wanted me, he started losing interest in the relationship. He wasn't as forceful. We continued to date until I had to come to a realization that he wanted only one thing from me.

Eventually we both pulled away and just weeks later I saw him with another woman at an outing. As they were bypassing me he looked at me and said, "Hello Jennifer", with such arrogance. It didn't hurt me but I was more disappointed than anything. It was a waste of my precious time and to lose my virginity to someone who I thought cared.

One year later, I decided to date again. I was dating my childhood sweetheart, Stacey. I have known Stacey since the age of 5. We had been friends for 15 years. Back in high school, Stacey and I went to prom together and that will forever be a special moment for me because he did not pressure me into doing things that I didn't want to.

Stacey and I had a horrible relationship. He had an arrogance about himself and he loved to engage in sexual activities. However, I did not always agree with engaging in it. He had some attractive qualities about himself on the outside but from the inside it didn't seem as genuine because he was always expecting something in return when he would give me things.

Only a few months into the relationship he cheats on me with his ex-girlfriend, Rhonda. My friend, Priscilla, walks up to me at work and says to me, "Jenn go and ask Stacey where he was hanging last night." Priscilla and Stacey's ex-girlfriend were neighbors.

I questioned him about it and he automatically knew who and where it came from. Priscilla walked up to me the next day after I confronted Stacey and she said "Jenn why did I almost lose my life last night?" Stacey threatened her and I felt really bad about what had taken place.

There were a lot of red flags about Stacey and after the incident with my friend being harmed by him, I began to slowly but surely release myself from him. It eventually led to a disinterest between the both of us and I was okay with that.

Stacey gives me a call to come over. I believed it was quite important due to the burial of his grandmother earlier that day. When I arrived, he had this strange sneaky look on his face and I asked if everything was okay. His response was "We're going to have to stop seeing each other."

I wasn't devastated or sad but more confused than anything. He explained how he was changing his life around and wanted a righteous life.

After he was done talking, I gave him my blessings and as I was walking off he was shaking his head as if I was supposed to be sobbing over the break up. As I was walking out the door his mother told me, "Goodbye and don't run off the road going home." I was shocked with her response and went on with my life.

A couple of weeks later after the break up my coworker Nancy pulled me to the side and said Jenn I got something to tell you. I said, "What?" She explained how Stacey and LaTasha had always been a couple, even while we were dating. She continued to say she told him to break up with you. LaTasha and I worked together at B-King but on different shifts.

After Nancy spilled the beans to me, I said "Stacey the so-called born again Christian who left me because he turned his life around?" She responded yes. She went on to say he's been buying her things and she's been telling us about their intimate encounters. I said "How was it possible I missed all of this?" Nancy said when he would pull up at the drive through where LaTasha takes the orders they would make sure to keep you occupied in the back to avoid coming up front to see them in action through the window.

I said to myself, "The nerve of him to use his grandmother as an excuse for his wrongdoing." At that moment, I was in shock with everything that had just taken place.

A few days later after his lies were exposed, he called me. Of course I didn't answer because he was left in the past and I didn't want to hear anything he had to say. I asked Nancy to tell LaTasha to tell Stacey to stop calling me. It was messy of me to do that but I was disgusted at both of them. LaTasha knew about me and Stacey's relationship.

My friend Priscilla told me not to worry about it because the two of them were just alike. She knew Stacey and LaTasha, personally. LaTasha loves what he loves and he got with someone who can give him just that.

Nancy went to LaTasha to tell her to tell Stacey to stop calling my phone. Latasha started sobbing and did not expect Stacey to treat her like that. She called his phone at the job and Stacey came walking through the door to prove his point.

When he walked up front to speak to LaTasha I was in the back but as he walked in we could see each other at a distance. I looked over at my other coworker Wonda and she was shaking her head saying wow this is so foul. Stacey continued to prove the type of human being he was. When he was done kissing up to his girlfriend he walked away and turned his head completely around the other way to avoid looking at me.

When he walked out LaTasha was all smiles. They told me Stacey was telling her that he didn't want me and that he was only calling to pick up his music he left behind which was another lie. I was dumbfounded due to his actions and in my opinion he'd become the most self centered hypocrite I've ever encountered.

After my experience with Stacey. I was done with people. I just couldn't handle the disrespect and rejection. I continued to attract the wrong people. I wasn't giving myself enough time to heal from my past. I needed to take a break from relationships and allow myself to heal properly.

I was so used to jumping in and out of relationships only to pay for it in the end. My mother called me the next day and I told her what Stacey had done to me and she said Jenn for someone to treat you like that it should be as if they never existed. She felt really bad about how I was treated and asked me to come live with her in Atlanta.

About a week later I packed my bags and moved to Atlanta Georgia. Moving to Atlanta was a breath of fresh air. My mother was in a nice spacious condo and I had my own room and bathroom so everything was looking pretty decent for the time being. Once I got settled I started looking for jobs and a week later I was hired at Panasonic.

Some of my time off I would go and stay with a family member on the outskirts of Atlanta. One weekend in the guest room relaxing I decided to go and take a shower before bed. As I was taking my shower, my family member's husband cracked the door and decided to take a sneak peek while I was taking a shower.

The lock on the door was broken and that's how he was allowed to open it. I pushed the curtains back, I screamed in complete shock, "What are you doing?" He makes up this lame excuse of having to use the restroom. I said "Go outside and use the restroom!" He then rushed outside to use the bathroom.

Once I stormed out of the house, he asked me where I was going to go and get something to eat. Of course my response toward him was only a few choice of words.

I got in my car and drove down the street and parked until my family member returned from running errands. Sitting there in the car, I couldn't stop reliving that moment. It was something I never experienced in life. Once I made it back she was pulling in their driveway and she noticed I was just sitting in the car with no type of movement and she walked up to the car and opened the passenger door and I spilled every last bean.

We walked in the house and nothing else was said. Hours later he arrived and I could hear him in the next room calling me crazy.

I could hear her telling him to be quiet and get into bed. I was dumbfounded because I just knew she would take my side.

I got up and started packing my bags. She walked in the room and told me she had to get up early in the morning and wanted me to wait until then to leave. I was shocked how easily she let him back in.

I went to a hotel the next morning and surprisingly she contacted me. I assumed she called every hotel until she was able to reach me because I did not tell her what hotel I was staying at. She avoided talking about the situation. The only negative thing she had to say about the situation was not for me to use profanity in her house. I was in disbelief! I continued to explain myself and she called me a liar and I hung up in her face.

When I got to work the next day, I spoke with one of my co-workers about the situation. I was hurting so bad. The hurt and pain was unbearable that I wanted to be alone and away from everybody.

Once I moved in with my roommate and got settled, I needed some time off from work. I was severely suffering from emotional damage. My social life was still popping and I continued to hang out with friends over the weekend.

This one particular friend I had was a female. Shanice was appealing to the eye. I was 22 and she was 47. We became closer after spending so much time with each other at work.

I became really drawn to Shanice on an emotional level. I began to feel this attraction I've never felt towards a woman. Besides being beautiful, she was drawn to me and that love I felt that was missing within me drew me closer and closer to the point of becoming desirable and lustful.

At that moment I began to question myself and without fully realizing at the moment I had already stepped into something I'd never dreamt of becoming.

Chapter 2

PAIN

Jeremiah 33:6

Nevertheless, I will bring health and healing to it; I will heal my people and will let them enjoy abundant peace and security

CHAPTER 3

With all the time I had on my hands, I chose to pursue my connection I had with Shanice. The pain I'd just encountered, thinking of Shanice gave me a reason to get up everyday with a smile on my face.

Overtime we'd become so close, our coworkers began to question our friendship. We deeply had an attraction for one another. I became jealous seeing her with other people and vice versa.

We grew close to one another each day but there was an obstacle in the way of what I was aiming to achieve. I'd ask her what she'd be doing the weekend and she'd always have to get back with me because she had this arrogant jealous boyfriend, Kerry. He was extremely jealous and controlling but it didn't stop me.

Surprisingly, she would turn him down and it created a distance between them once he saw how he couldn't keep us apart. I met Kerry once at her parents 50th anniversary celebration she was hosting. They actually made a beautiful couple but he treated her like crap. It was obvious due to his status. He was very wealthy but only chose to spend time with her when it was convenient for him.

Our first outing together we went to a restaurant and movie in Atlanta. I was opening and closing doors for her. At that moment I was ready to take things to the next level but deep down I knew it wasn't possible due to the age gap.

After spending the whole day together, I drove her home and she kissed me goodnight. The next weekend I met her sons, Ricky and Trey. Trey lived in Atlanta and Ricky lived in Chicago with his father. Ricky and I hit it off pretty good. I was drawn to him but only in a platonic way. Shanice picked up on our chemistry and she said okay Ricky that's your little sister and he said wow that just killed everything.

Shanice and I knew what was up with that. I wasn't going to take a step further with Ricky out of respect. We continued to date every other weekend. Eventually I grew bored of the situation due to not being active enough.

One day I decided to step outside of the connection and start mingling with other people. This guy Jake walks up to my station. Jake was very handsome. After we introduced ourselves he told me that he'd been watching me for a while and finally had the guts to come and say something to me.

I was pretty much over this fantasy with Shanice. I've always been this action type person and so I decided to do just that with Jake. He and I started off pretty good but emotionally I was still attached to Shanice. I couldn't help but to accept that I really dig this woman. She was all I thought about and being with Jake was a joy in some ways but overall a cover up.

I was in love with Shanice while dating Jake and I was an extremely confused individual that needed some type of an outlet. I didn't want to accept the fact that I was gay.

Jake and I decided to spend some time at his crib on a Friday after work. Being there cuddled up on the couch with him, I decided to stay the night. Once we got in bed and talked for a while he turned over to kiss me but I just didn't feel anything. We were attracted to each other but I couldn't get into it and I pushed him away.

I felt bad about pushing him away and I didn't want him to feel as if I was playing games with him. I was just so confused. He turned over and told me it was okay and we both fell asleep. I admired him for not forcing or getting upset.

The next day waking up and getting out of bed everything seemed to be just fine. He fixed us breakfast and we played video games until it was time for me to go to work.

When I arrived at work Shanice had an attitude with me. She wasn't saying anything to me. Her last words to me were, "Are you still with that boy? My reply was yes ma'am I am!

Later on that day at work Jake's attitude was different towards me and he was also distant. We had planned on spending some more time with one another later on that day along with him promising to take me to dinner.

I asked him what time we should meet up for dinner but he had to take a rain check. He gave me an excuse about doing something for his mother. I said oh really? He said yes I really have to see about her and run some errands.

I said okay well since you're dipping out on me then it's over. He said okay if that's what you want and it was over just like that. I said wow Shanice is mad and Jake is gone so what is it to do next?

After some emotional recovery for a few days, my mother gave me a surprise call. She asked me to move in with her. I hesitated but thought it couldn't be such a bad idea due to the loss of my job I'd been working at for the past couple of years.

I appreciated my mother for letting me stay with her until I got back on my feet. I applied for Subway and Holiday Inn. Both jobs hired me and it was up from there. I was a cashier at Subway and this guy who was managing the pizza place next to me would come in everyday to order two chocolate chip cookies.

One particular day he comes in to converse with me. He said hello, may I have two chocolate chip cookies and my name is Shamar by the way. I said hello "I'm Jennifer" He asked if I liked pizza and I responded, sure I love pizza. He said what kind do you like and I said pepperoni and he said okay I'll take care of that. As he walked away little did I know in the next few months my whole life was about to take the most drastic change.

Chapter 3

SEXUALITY
2 Corinthians 5:17

Therefore, if anyone is in Christ, he is a new creation. The old has passed away; behold, the new has come

CHAPTER 4

After Shamar offered to bring me a pizza from the store he was managing and me accepting, I didn't have this idea of getting to know him on a romantic level. I just needed someone to talk to on a platonic level. I definitely needed an outlet but only little did I know of what my life was about to become in just a couple of months.

Our first date we decided to go out to eat. Once we got to the restaurant and without hesitation, he explained his past relationship and how he was treated by his ex-girlfriend. The sound of it, she used him up pretty bad but again there is always two sides of the story.

I had this sudden feeling of making a huge mistake because I didn't want to mislead him in any way. This was just a simple hangout. Shamar seemed to be very intelligent and was a bit on the heavy side but I didn't want his appearance, due to my childish mentality to overtake wise decisions.

Going deeper into the conversation, I told him a little bit about my past relationships but chose not to get too deep because I didn't want him to get the idea of me looking forward to being in a committed relationship.

Some weeks later I start noticing a difference in Shamar's behavior. He was very arrogant and he'd come off as if I really didn't know much and his opinion of things were much wiser. The sad part about it is that he always ended up being wrong.

I made a decision not to get in a relationship with him but ended up doing just that. I felt if I leave him then I'm back to square one. Not feeling loved and just at a dead end in my life. I was holding so much in and I needed that emotional support, even with his wrongdoing.

About a couple of months into the relationship, on a Saturday night, we chilled at his crib and watched a few movies in bed. He wraps his arms around me and tells me he has never been able to do this with a girl. I said really? He said when I would try to cuddle with them they would tell me not to touch them. It really surprised me that Shamar allowed them to treat him that way because he was so outspoken and firm with everything else that he did in his life.

As we continue to watch television, Shamar raises up and excuses himself to go to the restroom. When he returned he knelt down and was searching for something under the bed. I said what are you doing? He raise up and pulls out this huge diamond ring.

I said what is this?! He said will you marry me? I hesitated due to shock and it being only two months into the relationship. Deep down I didn't want to marry him but on the flip said I was saying maybe I will grow to love him.

After some thought I said yes I will marry you. We walked to his mother in the next room and announced to her the big news but she didn't look too happy. Her only words to us was do y'all have the money? I expected her to feel that way but we continued with our decision.

We planned our wedding date a year from the date we got engaged. We both were pretty excited. I believe we were more excited about it being a show than us actually loving each other the proper way. We both married for the wrong reasons and I feel with the fact I was celibate, it pushed him a little further to go ahead and do it the right way.

I feel we both were trying to convince ourselves that it's the right thing to do despite all of the red flags that were in front of us.

I knew deep down I was about to make the biggest mistake ever. We both were anxious to leave the nest but only little did we know what would take place in the long run.

About a month prior to our wedding day we got our own place. I allowed him to move in alone until we were married. I wanted to do things the right way but there were so many other things that were out of order. Definitely on an emotional level.

A week prior to our wedding day we were making preparations, gathering family and church members from around the world who were attending. Once we arrived in my hometown for the meet and greet Shamar was amazed by the huge support system we had. Shamar didn't have many family members but my family on both sides were pretty large.

You can't imagine all the work we had to put in along with family members flying in from all around the world. After rehearsal dinner. I was ready to get home and get into bed. Once I got in bed I began to question myself heavily! I had thoughts about what will everyone think of me if I call this wedding off.

I was very unsettled in my spirit. Everything hit me at the last minute. My sister walked in the room and she looked at me with this strange look as if I needed to say something to her. It was like she could see through me without saying anything.

I wanted to express myself to her and that I wanted to call it off but I couldn't look like a fool to everyone that had made that sacrifice to be there and working extremely hard for things to be perfect.

The next day was the big day and I was extremely nervous! We pulled up and I went to the dressing room to get dressed and everything was so beautiful on the outside but I felt so empty on the inside.

My mother and sister were in the dressing room getting me dressed. Once we finished I walked out and went around the front of the church to meet up with the bridesmaids. I walked in and my aunt Drenda looked at me and said Jenn you are so beautiful and began to shed tears.

Once the party walked down the aisle, I could hear the musician playing, "Here comes the bride." My dad walks up to me and I grab his arm and he walks me down the aisle. I looked at Shamar and the whole wedding party and everything was so beautiful. It was so unfortunate because I wanted to feel like my surroundings.

Shamar looked very happy. He was showing every tooth in his mouth. After we became husband and wife, the musician played " Isn't She Lovely" by Stevie Wonder. Shamar grabbed my hand and we walked down the aisle and our guest threw rice from each side. On our way out the door, everyone was in tears and it was such a great thing to see.

After we took photos, we headed across the street for the reception. Everything was set up beautifully. Our host did such a great job along with our coordinator. We walked and everyone clapped and cheered on our way to the party table.

We had one of the hugest cakes you'd ever want to see at a reception and the fountain was flowing with wine along with a buffet and numerous gifts.

The reception was so much fun and it was like a family reunion with family I haven't seen in years from around the world. When it was time for me to throw the bouquet, my Aunt Sharon was hilarious. As always, she was grabbing and pushing everyone out of the way at every wedding reception.

After I threw the bouquet, Aunt Sharon flies in the air and snatches it out of another participant's hand and dives to the floor. Aunt Sharon has always put on a show and we were ready for it. Shamar was up next with his garter. Shamar threw his garter behind him and the group of men who participated moved back as it was approaching them and the crowd laughed hysterically.

We let the crowd close out with line dancing as we were walking out heading to the hotel to give ourselves away to one another. Once we arrived at the hotel room everything came down on us all at once.

We were wiped out! Once we got out of the shower and got into bed, Shamar looked at me and said okay honey let's give this a try.

I was a little nervous because I didn't know what to expect but we were married so whatever isn't up to par I'll just have to accept it and improve it, if needed. Once we got into the groove I was very disappointed but I chose not to be too harsh with my thoughts. It was no sexual chemistry whatsoever.

The next morning we got up and had breakfast before church service. We had church service at my home church and my church members from Atlanta attended as well. Once service started the pastor asked mom to get up and play the organ and mom called all of us up to sing with the choir. It was such a great feeling and it took us back to the old days.

After service we went across the street to the fellowship hall to eat and mingle with the congregation. The food was so delicious! One thing you can say about Louisiana is that you'll never be disappointed when it comes to cooking and eating.

After fellowshipping, Shamar and I said our farewells to everyone and headed back to my sister's crib to pack our things and head for the road. Once we arrived at our new place, Shamar had everything set up so neat and clean. It felt good to be on my own without someone looking over my shoulders.

A few months into the marriage things were going okay. We had a lot of cookouts and hangouts. We never had that chance living with parents and roommates the majority of our lives.

About six months into the marriage we were trying to have a baby. After trying for quite some time my stomach started growing. It was getting bigger and bigger by the day. We were very excited because there was no doubt in our minds that I was expecting. We were so sure to the point of not taking a pregnancy test.

Weeks after the swelling, my cycle appeared. I was dumbfounded! I told Shamar that my cycle was on and he became really worried. He said honey why is your stomach swelling the way that it is? I didn't have the answer but knew that I needed to get checked out immediately!

After visiting four doctors with no results, the last doctor decided to send me to a specialist. When I arrived at the specialist they did a thorough check up and I was praying to God for them to find something this time around. I didn't have a clue what was going on with me.

After waiting in the room for my results, the nurse called me in the room to speak with the specialist. I sat down and he said Jennifer, "What have you been so stressed about for this cyst tumor to swell up to ten pounds?" As I replied and was shocked at the same time I said, I had a very stressful wedding over a year ago and other things that were going on with me internally that I'd rather not discuss.

After telling him part of the problem I agreed on having the surgery. I really didn't have a choice because the tumor was constantly growing. It looked as if I was carrying a ten pound baby.

I broke the news to my family and I had the greatest support system. Everyone across the world was praying for me and I'm very thankful for everything because my recovery was a success!

A few months after my recovery, Shamar and I weren't getting along too well. I didn't have an opinion when it came to us building or doing whatever together as a husband and wife should. His attitude had just gotten worse over time and I was real close to just being over it.

Once we became financially stable, we moved into a bigger and better place. He was working for this transportation company that was long distance and shortly after he got his new job, I was hired at this food factory and we both were making pretty decent money.

My new job was amazing. The money was good and the people were really cool. A week later on the job, this female worker passed by me and I was like wow, she's attractive. She had this tomboyish style that was similar to mine and that drew me in instantly.

My boss introduced Nikki as our newest member. She walked over to me and introduced herself, personally. At that moment I felt something. Just days later we became really close. Working on the assembly line together was like we were the only two in the building that existed.

Chapter 4

CONFUSION

Matthew 9:36

When he saw the crowds, he had compassion on them because they were confused and helpless, like sheep without a shepherd

CHAPTER 5

It had been a month working at my new job and I was so in love. Nikki was very beautiful. She had long black silky hair with beautiful brown eyes, pretty white teeth and a milk chocolate complexion. That alone gave me reason to wake up every morning with excitement, heading to work.

When I would arrive to work I would make sure everything on me and around me was up to par before Nikki's arrival. Once I started my prep I knew within seconds she'd be appearing.

Her everyday routine after she clocked in would be helping me prep up my station and of course catch up on conversation and then she would head on over to her regular line.

Whenever she'd step away from me I could feel her watching me. We both felt just having those small conversations throughout the work day would eventually lead to something much greater. The chemistry was too strong for it not to.

I had this feeling over me as if I knew she was coming after me. It was only a matter of time. One Friday at work things began to take a shift. It started in our conference room at a party we attended with the rest of our coworkers.

I was sitting next to the guys and they were flirting with me. Nikki gave them this look like please you would not know what to do with that. I looked at her and then at them and just laughed it off. I had to maintain this image of being the perfect wife. I played really hard but I knew Nikki was about to change some things in my life.

After the party she comes over to ask me for my number. As I was writing the number down, I could feel the heat rushing through my hand. I gave her my number and she placed it in her pocket saying she could feel the heat and started laughing.

At that point it was too strong for anything to come in between what was taking place. We both walked outside to get some fresh air and I was so excited and anxious because it was the weekend and Shamar was on the road and it was the perfect time for us to get to know each other a little better outside of work.

As the weekend went by she didn't call me or anything. I thought she'd be really anxious to see me. Monday came along and she didn't show up for work. I had the impression something may have gone wrong. Tuesday morning she shows up with all smiles and I'm giving her this look like wow you could've called or something.

She walks over and gives me this excuse about being really busy and it was really no big deal. I knew she was a wild girl and a heavy club goer so I knew she was someone who I couldn't hold back.

Two months later, we were talking everyday and pretty much knew most things about each other. At this point curiosity had overtaken me and I'd do anything and everything to be with her. One Friday night being home alone and Shamar being on the road long distance, I was yearning for her company.

I decided to give her a call and she picked up with her usual seductive voice and I said "Hey can you come over?" Surprisingly she rejected me. She said Jenn I'm not ready to come over and there was complete silence between the two of us. I was confused by her response because I thought we both were anticipating this moment.

I said well, I'm really bored at home alone and would really like some company. She said okay but just for a little while. I had a feeling why she'd have second thoughts about moving forward because I was married and I'm sure she didn't want any confusion and getting caught up in a love triangle.

I went to pick her up from her crib and we came back to my place and sat down on the couch and watched a few films. We didn't make it through the third film after making her move.

I was completely gone. The devil had me right where he wanted me and the sad part is that I was fully aware of it. It was complete silence over a period of time after what had just taken place. I asked her what the silent treatment was all about and she asked me if I was sure about her being the first female I was intimate with and I said of course. I had no reason to lie about anything.

After our encounter, we had gotten so bold to the point of not caring what people thought of us in public. We were very comfortable and in love. I didn't care at all. All morals had been thrown out of the window. I really just wanted to be myself even if it included being dead wrong. I was even being bold enough to bring her around Shamar at this point and really not caring about how he felt about the situation.

When I introduced the two of them I told him that she was a good friend from work but in reality was my full blown girlfriend. The three of us spent a lot of days together. She was a massage therapist and would butter him up with massages from time to time and I believe that drew him in and allowed him to accept things that were going on between the two of us.

Nikki and I had a two year affair. We did so many things together as a couple. Her family knew about us and we were very open around them but my family only knew of her as a good friend. The second year became very rocky. She was a heavy drinker.

She was very honest about most things. She even confided in me about her cocaine habit. She was fresh out of rehab just weeks before we met. Along with the heavy drinking I had a feeling she had relapsed because I began to see major changes in her attitude.

One day I went through her phone to see if she was using drugs behind my back. Going through her text messages my suspicions were confirmed. She texted a male from work asking if he had some snow. Once I put two and two together I said okay this relationship is beyond over.

The situation became too much for me to handle. It was such a turnoff and I was beating myself up for allowing her to move in with me. The attraction was no longer there and it was no going back for me. My cold actions towards her made her behavior even worse.

The night when things took a turn for the worse was when I walked up to her drinking gin outside of my home. I told her repeatedly to not drink it around me because it made her crazy. I walked up on her drinking it inside her car and God knows what else. I asked her what she was doing and she stepped out of her car sloppy drunk and staggering.

I looked at her and everything hit me like a ton of bricks. I felt everything that I had done and thought I was getting away with was coming back tenfold.

When she stepped into the house sloppy drunk I asked her to leave. I knew it wasn't safe for her to drive but at this point nothing mattered to me but getting her out of there. I told her to leave and that it was over and she threw a major tantrum!

Screaming and yelling saying I knew you were going to break up with me. She came off as if she was the victim. She stormed up the steps and I stormed right behind her.

I walked up the stairway and into my room and there she was on the phone with her ex-girlfriend talking about me. That took it to another level of disrespect. I walked over to her and grabbed the phone out of her hand and broke it as I was grabbing it.

She called me every name in the book and then punched me in the eye. I'm in shock like yo what just happened? I hit the floor and she sits on top of me and continues to throw punches.

At this point I couldn't grab her and push her off of me. She came back for more and we continued to tussle. After she hit the wall, it was the end of that and she looked over at me and said let's stop before we kill one another.

She walked out of the room and I'm lying on the floor like God, what is this and what is happening to me? I've never dreamt that I would be caught up in a situation like this as an adult in my own place in a million years.

I was in too deep. Violence has never been my character. My life was definitely going downhill along with hers. I called her sister Levon begging her to come get her out of my house.

Levon calmed me down and told me to just let her sleep it off until the next morning. I went to my room and got into bed. Nikki made her way into the room later on that night and laid next to me.

The next morning the alarm goes off and I rise up in bed asking myself did this really take place last night in my own home? I looked over at Nikki and she stared at me with this look of sorrow once she noticed my face. She turned over and buried her face into the pillow.

I got up and went to the bathroom and looked in the mirror and I said no way I can go to work with this black eye. I called my boss and told him about my face and he told me that I had to come in anyway and to not worry about anything.

The both of us got dressed and no words were spoken. It was complete silence and I wanted it to continue that way. Nikki packed the rest of her things up and left. I left right behind her and headed off to work.

On my way to work I said God I know I'm reaping everything I've done with Nikki these past two years. Shamar and I weren't on good terms either. I no longer wanted to be in the marriage. We didn't have much for each other anymore. We were totally disconnected.

One day after work my car broke down. My friend Shane was nice enough to give me a ride until it was fixed. Shane and I worked the same shift and he stayed around the corner from us. Shamar didn't push to get the car fixed but made sure I didn't miss any days of work. When he saw Shane pull up to drop me off, it triggered him for some odd reason but on the other hand didn't try to help me find a way to work.

Once I got my car fixed, I started making preparations to leave the marriage. Shamar and I were two of the most self centered individuals and one of us had to come to the conclusion that one of us had to leave.

I remember breaking my hand at work and being out for two weeks. Shamar was fed up and demanded that I go back to work with a broken hand. Shamar and I were young and didn't understand the true meaning of a husband and wife duty. We walked into it thinking we were doing a good thing and things will improve over time but sadly we had to learn things the hard way.

My final decision to leave was when I overheard him talking to his friends saying he was going to trick me into doing something he felt was best to do for one of his other friends.

He brought it to my attention later on that day and he said Jenn we will be moving in with my friend and his girlfriend's house so we can help them pay their bills. He continued to say they're financially unstable at the moment.

I said I don't know them like that and why are we sharing our money with them? He said well this is what it is and what it's going to be. I said okay and walked off. That was the last conversation for me. The next day he went to work and I packed my things and left everything else behind and didn't look back.

I told him that I no longer wanted to be in the marriage and that I will be staying with my mother. I sort of felt bad about the way that I did things. I didn't tell him face to face but instead sent him a text while he was on the job long distance.

I didn't get a text or a call back until weeks later. He wanted to talk about mending things. When we met up the first thing to come out of his mouth was honey I thought I was going to have to get out there and start dating again. I gave him this side eye look as if you think it's going to be that easy?

His friend Ron comes over to join us and makes a statement about how choked up Shamar was over me and how he had to stay with him and his lady for a few weeks to get over me. I was like wow he was that choked up and didn't attempt to call me? Ron replied well I thought he was calling you and I said no sir he was not calling me. I felt Shamar was being really fake and wanted his friends to think he didn't have a clue what went wrong behind closed doors. Shamar clearly knew our marriage had been dead for years.

After our meet up I officially knew it was over. I was certain I made the right decision. A week later, Shamar called and asked if we decided to make it work, could I put the car in his name. I said no way. Everything we had was in his name while we were together and he used that against me everytime we had an altercation and after I rejected his request that was our last conversation.

I ran into Shamar's brother's girlfriend at the dollar store and she made a statement about his mother crying everyday and couldn't believe that I did it that way. I'm sure he painted this perfect picture of himself to make me look bad.

A year later he called and I looked at my phone and was quite surprised! We were still legally married so I decided to pick up. He said yeah I got some papers for you to sign and I asked, "Where do you want to meet up?"

We both agreed to meet in Union City at Shoney's restaurant. He and a female friend pulled up behind me and I said would you like to go inside and sign and he said no with an attitude. I got the papers and drove off.

I drove off and I was like wow he will never grow up and what's the attitude for? We weren't checking up on each other and I felt everything should've been cool. The next day the deal was sealed between the both of us. No spousal support or anything, slate clean.

Months later after I stacked a pretty good grip of my money up, Nikki and I were still in touch and I was desperate for a roommate. I was extremely anxious about leaving my mother's crib but was still unsure if moving in with Nikki would be the wisest decision.

She was still in that lifestyle that I'd pulled away from. I was getting right with God and getting back into his word. One day she called me and insisted on moving in with her. Eventually I agreed and once I moved in and got settled, I felt I'd made a great decision.

It was a very nice place and neighborhood. In the beginning everything was good. We didn't go back down memory lane or any of that extra stuff and she tried at times but I felt it was best to keep things strictly platonic. I was moving on to big and better things in life. I was working at the post office and had a few friends who I'd hang out with during the weekends. I was living a clean life and striving to keep myself rooted in Christ until one day this female Sybil changed everything that surrounded me.

Chapter 5

ADULTERY

1 John 1:9

If we confess our sins, he is faithful and just and will forgive us our sins and purify us from all unrighteousness

CHAPTER 6

Sybil was an attractive woman that every dude was trying to get at on the job. The first day I saw her I thought she was stuck up and trying to take over everybody's position. She had extreme controlling issues. The first two months with her being on the job she'd come up to me and chat for a little bit.

She was very seductive and eventually I started feeling those old desires creeping back in my spirit. One day during break, a group of us were discussing my birthday celebration that was right around the corner. Sybil walked towards us and asked if she could join us. Of course I said yes. I was a little excited but she was feeling this much younger guy on the job.

Twan was closer to her son's age. She had a man at home as well and all of us were aware of it but she had this spirit on her that would suck you in and I was one of those victims. I couldn't shake it. I had gotten so attached and wanted to get closer and closer.

At this point in my life I had been celibate for quite some time and just trying to do the right thing overall. When Sybil appeared the first day on the job, I felt that she was going to become some type of distraction. If not me, someone else for sure.

The night of my party, we met up at the bowling alley in Atlanta. Everyone I invited showed up and more. Sybil was there and so was Twan. Her focus that night was more on him than me. Nikki was with me and we rolled together but my focus was Sybil to be quite honest.

We bowled and drank all night. It had been my first alcoholic beverage in years. I had broken all kinds of rules at this point. My mission for God was completely destroyed.

I was watching Sybil all night and amazed at how she was extremely comfortable giving Twan lap dances in front of everyone. I said wow! She is really out there and off the chain with it!

The end of the night all of us got together and took professional photos and I must say it turned out to be one of my best celebrations. The next day Sybil and I hooked up to go see a horror movie. It was an innocent date night.

After the movie I drove her to her car and we went our separate ways. When we returned to work the next week, she had this glow about her as she was approaching me. I said go on somewhere before your little boyfriend gets upset.

Sybil would go from my station to Twan's station throughout the whole day and sad to say she had the both of us right where she wanted us, in the palm of her hand.

A few weeks passed and I noticed a difference between the two of them. She was pulling away from him and pursuing me more each day. We had become so close to the point of people hesitating to approach one without the other on the job. They thought we were an item but it was strictly platonic. It was more of an infatuation on my end and I just loved seeing her defending and jumping down people's throats about me if she felt I was being mistreated in some type of way. She was very attentive and possessive.

Sybil was nine years older than me and that's what I continued to attract. I was attached to older women and it filled a temporary void from not feeling loved over the years and having that attachment always led to this obsession of a pull I wasn't able to shake.

Sybil and I weren't explicit with one another but we did have our cozy moments. Her boyfriend Zard didn't care for me too much in the beginning. When I'd be at their crib he would block me in certain areas or simply give me this signal being king of the castle.

He didn't trust me or Sybil and he knew it was something special about our connection. Sybil was more of a protector than anything else. I was very timid and she was always there to pick up the pieces. Shortly after getting to know me, me and Zard became cool and the three of us would even hangout together from time to time.

One night the three of us decided to go out and hangout at his motorcycle club gathering with his boys. Sybil rode with me and Zard took off on his motorcycle. On the way there she told me she had been thinking about me a lot lately and she couldn't figure out what was going on with her. I was like hmmm are these two trying to set me up for later on tonight?

I feel we both had feelings for one another but decided to keep things clean. Most of her time was spent with me. More with me than her own family. While hanging out at the sports bar we decided to go club hopping on the same strip. She threw up the deuces to Zard and we went on our merry way.

When we got to the club I bumped into a couple of friends from my past and we partied with them for a few hours and headed back. When we returned to the sports bar Sybil walked over to Zard and whispered something in his ear and she looked over at me and asked me if I was ready to leave and I said sure let's roll out.

When we made it back to the crib Zard was already there. I said there is no way he made it back before us. Whatever they had setup was not the game plan on my end. When we walked in the house Zard was already upstairs. Sybil walked over to me and asked me if I was comfortable and I said sure and she walked off and went upstairs. Minutes later she returned quite revealingly. She walks over to me and bends down and gives me a kiss goodnight.

Our connection lasted for about a solid two years. Everything was going pretty good until this young guy Austin appeared in her life. He was one of the drivers on the job and I would see them talking everyday and noticed she was giving him quite a bit of attention on her lunch breaks.

I asked her if anything was going on and she denied any type of activities outside the job. Austin was a cool dude but I could see he was madly in love with Sybil. It was obvious they had a thing going on and the closer she got to Austin the more she changed towards me.

The more I saw them together the more unsettled I felt. I said let me go and get a life and stop running up behind these women with all of their baggage. Once I started associating with other coworkers on the job some were noticing the distance between me and Sybil and decided to approach me. This guy Len was one of those coworkers.

It had been three years since I'd dated a guy. Len would bring me food everyday until he decided to take it up a notch and asked me out to have dinner with him. He took me to this Italian restaurant and we hit it off pretty well. Len was very charming and giving.

Len wanted to take things a little further with me and I decided to do just that. He was very reserved and that was a plus for me. I spent the weekends with him before I made the final decision to move in. One morning while eating breakfast Sybil gives me a surprise call.

I pick up the phone and Sybil says Jenn where are you? I've been trying to reach you and I said I'm at Len's and before I could say anything she hung up on me. She was furious with me which I couldn't understand because she had already made the choice to spend her time with other people.

As Len and I became closer over the months I began to notice he had major trust issues. He was accusing me of something every time I stepped out the door. I was furious at being accused of something I wasn't doing.

One of those incidents led to an argument and at that point I'd had enough. I started packing my bags and on my way out the door he grabs me from behind and pulls me down to the floor and wraps his legs around me.

I'm screaming telling him to let me go! I called Sybil and told her I was being held hostage and she said do I need to call the police? After he heard her through the phone he released me and I went on my merry way.

I stayed over at Sybil's house until I calmed down. Len called me over the weekend and apologized for his actions. Monday morning Len and I walked in together at work. Sybil was running mail through the machine. I walked over to her to say hello and she said wow are you back with him?! I said yes we worked things out over the weekend.

She was so upset for some odd reason. She had this whole other life that she gave to while giving me so little. She turned around towards Len and called him every name in the book.

I walked off before things got out of hand and I bypassed Len and told him that we'll talk later on. Len texted me once I made it to my work area and he had a few choice of words for her as well and I told him to keep calm and that what she thought didn't matter and that I was moving forward with him and I did just that.

Len and I were talking about marriage and building a future together. I wasn't head over heels in love but was content due to him being quite reserved. He was definitely a homebody which was a great thing and I became pretty reserved due to his actions.

One day at work I began to feel sick. I was throwing up along with having a missed period. I walked over to Len's station and told him I was sick and that I haven't seen my period in months. He looked at me and laughed and said you are really in denial aren't you?

I left work early to go and take a pregnancy test. Once I got home I rushed to the bathroom and took the test and within seconds I was in disbelief! I said no way is this possible because I tried so hard in my previous marriage.

Deep down I knew I wasn't ready on a spiritual, mental, emotional or even a physical level but I knew once my child was born he would be loved unconditionally.

I was depressed but trying my best to push forward. I was still emotionally attached to Sybil. I began to question God because I didn't understand what I was feeling. Some days I would be good and then there were other days being very unhappy.

Len and I got married a few months before our son Case was born. When Case arrived he was my most ultimate joy. It took my mind off things that were irrelevant and just weighing me down. I was so thankful to God that he came out a healthy baby due to my mental and health state. I was extremely sick during my whole pregnancy.

Once my son turned a year old I went back to work. The post office welcomed me back and it wasn't the ideal job at the time but we needed that extra income temporarily. Sybil was my supervisor and it was a little dangerous for me to return and work under Sybil due to my feelings but I had to press through and wake up and smell the coffee. I was a wife and a mother and needed to get a grip of life.

In the beginning things were okay between Sybil and I. We were taking our lunch breaks together and just having a good time and making money together with no strings attached. She had strictly men working under her and once I came in and they started giving me a little attention, in the most respectful manner, her energy changed towards me.

One day after clocking in the guys were conversing and setting up the lineup for us to run the mail. I walked off to go get a soda out of the vending machine and I noticed I was fifteen cents short. Derrick offers to give me some change and Sybil is looking at us and walks over to me and grabs my hands and twists it around.

I blacked out! I was screaming and yelling and calling her every name except a child of God. Roderick and Derrick got me by the arm and walked me to the break room. I busted through the doors and the janitor asked me what happened. I said that Sybil put her hands on me.

He automatically knew who it was because everyone on the job knew we had history together. Once I cooled off in the breakroom and the janitor gave me some encouraging words to get through the night, I walked out the breakroom, grabbed my keys and bag without saying one word.

When I returned to work the next day I didn't plan on working. I had a plan to clock in and go to the general manager about the situation. When I got to the machine to prep mail, she walked past me saying what I need to be doing and I said first you're not going to keep talking to me like you don't have any sense.

I told Sybil that I wasn't done with her and I was going to report her for putting her hands on me. I walked off and went to the general manager. I told him everything and asked him to move me to the 1st shift. He told me that the supervisor would have to release me and I said no I have the upperhand to be moved regardless because she put her hands on me.

He said okay we'll have a meeting. He didn't take it seriously because he knew that me and Sybil, in the past couple of years, went through the storm and the rain together. I believe he just didn't want to get in the middle but I was over the foolishness. I wasn't going to allow her to have me quit my job. She was going to be gone before me and I had the evidence to prove it.

After I talked to the general manager I returned to my line and Sybil said with a soft calm voice, come here Jenn. I walked over and she made up this cry and said Jenn I will never do anything to hurt you and you know that I love you. I was like wow this woman needs an oscar for this performance. Reality had started to kick in because she knew I wasn't playing with her.

She said what do you need and want me to do? I said I would like to go to the 1st shift and she told me okay with no hesitation. The next day I was on 1st shift and it was a breath of fresh air.

The 1st shift was perfect because it gave me time to spend with my family throughout the day. One day as I was running my mail through the machine, this female driver on the job Kate came over to drop some mail off for me to run. Little did I know I was headed for one of the most dangerous downfalls that I've ever experienced.

Chapter 6

DEPRESSION
Philippians 4:8

Finally, brothers and sisters, whatever is true, whatever is pure, whatever is lovely, whatever is admirable - if anything is excellent or praiseworthy - think about such things

CHAPTER 7

The first week on my job went pretty well and it was so peaceful with not having to run into unnecessary drama. This machine they had me working on was one of the areas the drivers come to drop off mail for the operators to run. Kate was one of those drivers who I'd come in contact with daily and she was so funny to me. She had this extremely high pitched voice I've ever heard on a female.

She would come by and drop mail off and crack a joke and go on about her day. She was very nice, built with a dark, chocolate complexion and very private. She stayed in her own lane and I admired that about her. You'd rarely see that from anyone working there. Everybody knew everybody's business.

Weeks passed and Kate would make her way back to the other position I worked at which was in the back of the warehouse. I noticed she was very talkative when I worked alone and it was a good thing because I enjoyed chatting with her. One day she walked in the back where I was working talking to someone on her phone and after hanging up from them she asked if I'd love to go out with them to a gathering and I said sure where are we going?

She mentioned a seafood spot down the street from her crib and I said okay and she goes on to say after that spot we will head on over to the strip club. I said really? It's not that I was a stranger to strip clubs, I just didn't expect for someone to invite me to something so exotic on the first outing.

We met up for dinner at the crab shack and ordered a few pounds of crabs and we talked and got to know a whole lot more. Her other friend Sheryl wasn't able to join us for dinner but met us later on that night.

Kate wasn't really my cup of tea due to her age. My preference was older women so she was actually the first to change that. I saw a different side of her hanging outside of the job and I was quite pleased. She was very bubbly and adventurous. After dinner we went to her crib to meet her friend before we attended the strip club. As we were sipping on wine relaxing on the couch she questioned me about Sybil.

She said are you and Sybil together? I said no. She said are the two of you cordial? I said no Sybil is old news. The crazy part of our conversation is that she didn't question me about my marriage or even my child that she knew about.

I gave Kate the full story about what happened between Sybil and I and she said wow she really is crazy and too old to be behaving the way she does. I said you are right and I have nothing else for her after she put her hands on me at the workplace in front of a mixed company.

Sybil was the type that could never control her emotions and always made it known to everyone that she mixes her business with pleasure and a behavior like that shouldn't definitely be in management.

After discussing Sybil for over an hour, Sheryl pulls up and honks her horn for us to come out and head to the strip club. We pulled up at the Flame and partied with the chicks for about three hours and called it a night.

When I got home Len and Case were knocked out. I went and took a shower and got into bed. Once I laid down, Kate was on my mind heavily. I knew she was someone who I really wanted to move forward with in friendship.

When I got to work Monday I was feeling good and anxious to see Kate walk through the door. She was different and young and that was very challenging for me. I've always loved a great challenge.

When she walked through the door and walked up to my station she asked me what I wanted for my birthday. I said I'm unsure and with my son being just two years old I can't go on a getaway trip unless he's in the mix.

She said okay just let me know something once you decide and I said I'll make sure I do that. The day of my birthday we decided to go out for breakfast before work. I pull up to her place, knock on the door and she opens the door and invites me in.

After getting dressed she walked up to me and placed my gifts next to me. She gives me this fashionable bag and a pair of boots. I was very appreciative with so little time we've known each other.

After I opened my gifts I walked over to her and she said " Jenn are you about to kiss me? I said yes I am. She started laughing and said give me a minute. She sits down on the edge of the tub rocking back and forth singing "Blessed assurance" and I said girl something is really wrong with you, there's no way possible you are this shaken up over a kiss.

Once we were done playing around we packed our things and headed out for breakfast. Once we got to the restaurant and got seated, we conversed about what to be expected from one another in the upcoming future. I couldn't give her much because I had another life.

We pretty much had an understanding about everything and there were no secrets, at least I thought at the time anyway. As we were conversing we had flapjacks, eggs, bacon and orange juice. Once we were done with breakfast we had to rush out to get to work on time.

After leaving work I went to daycare to pick up my baby boy. My son is my joy! I had all this love for my son but it was still a disconnection as the way a mother and wife should morally act inside and out. I was so confused internally to the point of not really caring about what I was putting out in the atmosphere.

Len and I were living in separate bedrooms and that created a major distance between us. He stayed to himself a lot and I believe he was dealing with past issues as well that he was battling. Most days it would just be me and my son in one room and he'd be in another and I felt it has to be much more to life than this.

Over a period of time me and Kate's relationship grew pretty strong but things began to change when this new guy Brandell appeared on the job. I started noticing a change in her and I was picking up on her keeping a close eye on him.

When I'd walk away from my station to the warehouse area, I would see her at his line smiling and talking and that was odd to me because Kate didn't deal with nobody but me on a personal level at the workplace.

I became very jealous of Brandell. I could see that she was really into him. On my way out the door leaving work one day I bypassed them talking at his line and got her attention to let her know we'll talk later.

I didn't get a call from her that night which was strange because we talked every night. The next morning she called me and said, "What are you doing? I said getting ready for work. She went on to say you may have to come and pick me up but don't come just yet, wait until I call you.

We hung up from each other and I said something doesn't sound right with this situation and I'm about to get to the bottom of it. I said let me hurry up and get there so I can see what's going on with her.

I pulled up to her subdivision and my suspicions were confirmed. Brandell's car was parked on the side of her crib. I was furious! I was honest with her about everything but she didn't do the same with me and because of that, the bond was broken.

I called her phone and she picked up and before I could say anything she said where are you? I need you to come and pick me up.

I said tell your little boyfriend Brandell that spent the night with you to take you.

After she was busted we just held the phone and it was straight crickets for a long period of time. I said I thought you don't allow anyone to come to your house Kate? Still crickets and she finally says whatever and I said yeah whatever and hung up.

I pull up to the job and as I'm walking in the building I'm completely out of it. I was completely in another world. I said everything keeps repeating itself.

Kate walks through the door and clocks in and she has this craziest look on her face. I'm like yeah that's that busted look. I went over to question her about what I'd seen and she gave me the same story. Nothing happened and they're just friends.

Just weeks after finding out about Brandell she slowly revealed to me about seeing another female. I said oh my God this is one huge soap opera. I didn't exclude my actions because they were bad as well and may have been worse due to me being a married woman.

Kate's girlfriend Ashton was in the palm of her hand. Ashton worshiped the ground she walked on. When I would see them together and observe things I would say wow Kate and I are two of a kind, not caring about anyone's feelings but our own.

Ashton was coming up to our job to visit her but Kate didn't care how that would make me feel or look due to the strong connection we had there for the past two years.

It was devastating to learn that Ashton was moving to Georgia from Alabama to live with Kate to attend the university. I went into a deep depression without fully realizing it at the moment.

It was some kind of way I needed to get my mind off of the situation. Driving to take my mind off of things I was led to this shop. I walked in searching for the unknown until I ran into this tall beautiful tool and it was a hookah. I picked it up and purchased it immediately.

This hookah became my best friend. I was indulging in it daily. I was inhaling more than exhaling, blindly destroying myself. Kate was over me. That was very hard for me to accept. Ashton became the center of her life and gave her things that I couldn't give because of my other life and that left me heartbroken.

Kate called me to go out with her to celebrate her cousin's birthday bash. I was somewhat uncomfortable about accepting the invitation because I needed that time to myself to avoid her at all cost.

I ended up accepting the invitation and met her at her place. I had this very strange feeling over me the entire night being with her. We arrived at the party scene and I said to Kate I have this funny feeling about going inside and I think it's best we don't go inside. She said I don't want to go in either but I need to go in and show support but we won't stay long.

I hesitated but decided to go ahead and support as well. We walked in together and the atmosphere was pretty cool due to it not being my cup of tea which is being in the midst of a club.

I ordered a hookah and a beer and we danced and smoked hookahs the entire stay. On our way out the door I felt pretty good but still had this feeling of being warned about something before I walked in.

On our way back to her place we were in the middle of a conversation and my mind went completely blank. Once I snapped back I asked her what we were just discussing and she looked at me real strange and repeated what was mentioned.

After dropping her off at the crib I still felt a little strange but continued to drive. About a block away from her crib I was driving in circles. I didn't know where I was and I said Jesus please take the wheel. I called her and there was no answer so I continued to drive.

I snapped back and realized where I was and hit the expressway. I was praying hard! I said Lord , please get me home safely. Once I got off the exit and made a right turn I pulled up to the traffic light and before making a complete stop I realized I was on the opposite side of the road.

I swerved back into the correct lane and once I made a complete stop everything turned black. I screamed and went into complete shock. I was stretched out over the passenger seat and my body was stiff as a board! I started praying again, Jesus please get me home and I snapped out of it.

I raised up and God gave me just enough strength to drive to my place that was right around the corner. Driving home my heart was beating extremely fast and I was having hot flashes and I knew just within moments I was going to die.

Once I pulled up to my place I said this was nothing but the power of God's hands getting me home safely. I walked in the room to tell Len what was happening to me and my son walked in staring at me and I was terrified because I had no clue what I was experiencing.

Len googled my symptoms but couldn't match what I was experiencing. As we were looking up different things to help my situation I had another attack. I rushed outside and ran around the entire building. Once I made it back inside the house I felt a little better.

I laid down on the couch and I said finally it's over. As I was drifting off another attack hit me and it felt as if I was losing oxygen. My face was stiff and my mouth was shifting from side to side and it felt as if something demonic had taken over me.

I said someone is spiritually doing something to me? I felt it was much more than over indulging in hookahs and alcoholic beverages. I got up and Len drove me to the hospital down the street. I screamed all the way there due to the multiple attacks I was having back to back.

We got to the hospital and I told them the issue and while waiting to be seen I was hallucinating the entire time. I was hearing voices and all types of other crazy things going on with me.

Once they examined me they couldn't find anything. The nurse told me that I'd escaped something major due to the symptoms. She prescribed me pain medication due to the major migraines I was experiencing.

When I arrived home I was feeling quite fine until later on that night. It felt as if someone placed a bag of hot coal on the top of my head. I was in severe pain!

In and out of the emergency rooms for two months they recommended me to set up an appointment to see a psychiatrist. My regular doctor eventually prescribed me antidepressant medication. I couldn't handle the medication due to the brain zaps. It was pure torture!

When I returned to work my boss and coworkers were praying for me on a daily basis. I really didn't have to say much for them to realize I wasn't myself. Some days I was barely combing my hair. I was completely out of it. Some days I would even walk off the job without giving my boss any notice. I'd go to my car and rest before taking off.

I would look at my son and say I cannot fail you. God please get me through this. I didn't know how I was going to make it. I felt with every inch of my soul the devil was trying to take me up out of here.

I was in my car one day after taking my daily walk and I said God I can't take this anymore. It's been two months straight enduring consistent pain and memory loss and I'm tired! As I was laying on my headrest in my car I felt this thump on my forehead and I raised up and was led to walk around the building again and pray.

I continued to do that on a daily basis along with eating healthy and drinking water. It was nothing but the grace of God that pulled me out of that situation and I was so thankful to God because he made it all possible.

After feeling so free and blessed I decided to pursue this basketball dream of mine that had been in my heart for the past few years.

It was this basketball community event I dreamt of achieving and I had every person in mind who I wanted to be a part of it. I began to make phone calls and as I was succeeding with my plans my son became very ill.

It started off with a minor cold for a couple of days but on the third day things took a turn for the worse. It started off a mild fever and about 1a.m. the smoke detectors were going off in the kitchen. I checked everything in the house and everything was clear, no fire inside or outside of our home.

I walked back in the room where my son was sleeping and checked his temperature and it was through the roof! Nothing was helping to bring it down. I went and told Len that something isn't right and that I need to take him to the hospital.

They examined him and they told me it was just a simple cold and to continue to give what I was giving him but I still felt unsettled due to his abnormal heart rate and an extremely high fever. Getting ready to pack up our things another nurse walked in and asked them if they could do an x-ray and once we got the results they pointed out a spot on his lungs.

Once they mentioned pneumonia I was dumbfounded! I said pneumonia!? At that moment I felt there was a major attack on my family and by me making it through the enemy was upset! After my son was extremely sick in the hospital for two weeks and pulling through it made my faith stronger and I said God you did it again!

Once my son got well I continued the plans for my dream event. I called my dad and our hometown basketball coach to have it held at the high school all of us attended.

I was getting ready to make contact with one of my greatest female inspirations. Rachel is an inspired athlete from all around and I felt it would be a true honor to have her to be a part of it. We were born and raised in Bastrop and attended the same high school.

I was in complete awe of her and loved to watch her play basketball growing up. I messaged her on facebook but we didn't have any type of connection with one another. Once I messaged her I became very anxious and nervous. Days went by without a reply and I said okay maybe she doesn't accept random messages from people.

One day in the restroom at my job I hear my facebook message ringtone going off. I picked up my phone and there it was, a message from Rachel. I froze up and I said what am I going to say to this woman? I clicked on the message and as I read it she was expressing to me about the warm and heartfelt message I sent her and being so thankful for it.

She told me she'd love to be a part of my event and to keep in touch with her. A couple of weeks later we were verbally talking about the plans I had lined up. We talked quite often and I wanted to know more and more about her.

I became mesmerized and was just loving so much of her company to the point of getting so caught up and placing the mission on the backburner. Along with that and making business moves, things became quite heavy on my shoulders. I was connecting with business people and it was hard to keep up with everything and I was in need of some type of guidance.

Praying to God was limited because I knew I wasn't doing things that were pleasing in his eyesight. I began to catch feelings and fully knowing this consistent behavior is an abomination to God. My fleshly desires were pulling more and more towards her and by doing these things I chose to seek other spiritual advice instead of the Most High God. I became very self-absorbed and eventually that led me down a very dark and gloomy path.

I was introduced to tarot reading through one of my devices. I was very curious with the colors and images on the cards and to be able to predict your future by clicking on that particular card. I clicked on the site for a future reading and just like that I was hooked and became quite possessed.

Chapter 7

MENTAL BREAKDOWN
Psalm 34:17-18

The righteous cry out, and the Lord hears them; he delivers them from all their troubles. The Lord is close to the broken-hearted and saves those who are crushed in spirit

CHAPTER 8

I felt the urge to do a tarot reading to see all of the plans I had lined up for my future endeavor. I asked the spirits about me and Rachel's connection in the near future due to us becoming closer everyday. We just had respect and admiration for one another and became attached quite fast but couldn't get close physically due to long distance. She lived in Baton Rouge and I lived in Atlanta. Our first time meeting each other in person was phenomenal!

The day before we saw each other we got into this small altercation over the phone about her not meeting me when expected. I pulled up to the hotel in our hometown and gave her a call to see how far she had gotten and she told me she had trouble leaving.

She said I will have to meet you tomorrow morning. I said well I wish I would've known that before I spent money for two nights at this hotel. I said by the way, you can come pick up your sister's gift at the front office and don't bother coming to my room.

She replied with boldness! She said It's a good thing I'm driving! Later on that night we talked things out and she showed up the next day as promised. The next morning I was very excited and a little disappointed because here I am about to meet one of my favorite people in the world but my dream event wasn't coming to fruition as planned.

Again here I am having that same attraction for women and wanting God to bless me while doing things that were so displeasing in His eyes. It was so disrespectful towards God and sincerely knowing he just brought me out of a deadly situation.

The unhealed flesh of mine yearned for more each day. Rachel made it to town and we met up at Ihop to get something to eat. As I was walking inside the restaurant to get us a table I heard this voice saying Jenn? I knew it wasn't Rachel's voice and so I looked to the right and both of my aunts were staring at me and I walked over in shock saying hello to Aunt Deb and Aunt Ree.

I was like gosh this is not the time! Rachel is on her way here and I'm in town and didn't tell a soul. Aunt Deb said we were just with your father and you haven't talked to him? I said no, Rachel and I are in town on business.

Rachel walks in and I look at her and she gives me this look like okay you aren't going to jump for joy? I really wanted to but was totally distracted. I walked over to her and gave her a nice friendly hug and introduced her to my aunts.

The waiter walked over to tell them that their table was ready and both of them said come on girls and join us for breakfast. We sat down at the table and I knew we were in for a treat because both of my aunts are hilarious! They questioned Rachel from left to right and Aunt Deb decided to ask her if she had any kids and Rachel looked at her almost spitting her drink out and replied no with a smile.

They asked her about her occupations and were quite impressed. Rachel is very well respected in the sportsworld and the community. After my aunts said their goodbye's, Rachel turned around and looked at me and she said okay Jenn! Does your aunt know you are a lesbian?

When I pulled up on you today I could definitely see it. I couldn't do anything but laugh. Once we got outside I walked over to her and gave her the tightest and longest hug ever! I was so happy to see her in person up close. Once we got done playing around we departed from each other and I drove back to the hotel and she went to go help her sisters put up the decorations for her sister's baby shower where we will meet up later that day.

I got to my room and chilled out for a couple of hours until it was time to meet up with Rachel and her family. She has seven sisters and all of them are extremely professional women. Her father at the time was our mayor in our hometown and I'm actually classmates with one of her sisters and played ball with her in middle school.

I had the chance to mingle with them at the shower and I had a pretty nice time. Rachel and I snuck out for a little while to go play ball with the guys who attended the shower. It was such a great feeling to be playing basketball with her and I must say she still had it.

Chapter 8

NEW AGE
Acts 19:18

Many of those who believed now came and openly confessed what they had done

CHAPTER 9

I'd become very bold with using tarot cards online. Bold enough to tell people the way they should or shouldn't be living if the spirits did or didn't approve of it. I would even discuss to Rachel certain readings I did on her and if I was a little skeptical about something, I was woman enough to question her about it.

Experiencing tarot I began to notice certain gifts that I had. I've known since a little girl that God had given me a certain kind of special spiritual gift and experiencing the dark realm for the wrong purposes that gift was awakened. I was heavily involved in divination.

Another thing that I began to realize using divination was that Rachel was connected to a dark demonic force behind the scenes. I was getting numerous visions about this demonic male coming after me. I had my spiritual advisor keep track of all of my steps and she'd mentioned to me that this very evil man was out to harm me but not to worry because I was covered.

This guy was revealed in one of my dreams. In this dream she and I were at this random gym she was recruiting at and I noticed this guy was staring at us and I tapped her on the shoulder to get her attention but she didn't turn around. She was too focused on her work.

I walked off and he followed me out the door. Once I made it out of the building he stepped out in front of me asking where I was going and I told him I had to go and catch my train and before I could get away his eyes lit up with fire. I woke up terrified!

In the dream he looked normal but after being awakened it was clear I was battling a demon. It was obvious in this situation that it was time to leave it behind because my mission is somewhere else and that I needed to press forward before I missed the ride, even in the midst of obstacles.

One Sunday morning at church the bishop was praying over me and he told me that it's finished. He said Jesus got you in the palm of his hand. I was like, is something about to happen to me or around me? Kate called me just days later and says to me I'm just calling because my Godsister who's a minister told me to tell you that God put it on her heart to say you are going to go through this storm and that it is some type of mission you are trying to accomplish but God says don't worry because he got you in the end.

Kate said I had to call you and tell you that and I was telling my Godsister that I hope nothing is going to happen to my friend. I became extremely nervous! I had just gotten a similar revelation from the Bishop just days prior.

After hearing those revelations I was still attached to Rachel. The battle I went through being attached to her was tough but at the same time I couldn't blame her for other people's actions.

One morning getting out of bed I was full of emotions about everything that was surrounding me and I decided to text her to get some things off my chest. I talked to her about the threats, the spiritual and physical attacks. One thing I can say is that she didn't discredit most things I mentioned to her but she chose not to speak on it due to dark forces.

I cared about her as a friend and wanted to protect her the best way I knew how. Eventually, I had to accept that it was a lost battle. After sending her the cryptic message about being attacked, they decided to turn it up a notch.

My property at my job was vandalized when I made it back to work, family photos were torn down and the cyber attacks had gotten worse as well. I definitely had to come to this conclusion that this was an old or current affiliation of hers working behind the scenes. After everything that had taken place I believe we both felt it was best to part ways from one another.

At this point I began to question God because I didn't feel covered in any type of way but had to realize I had put Him on the backburner and made up my mind to put total trust in other gods. My trust was in psychics, tarot cards and horoscopes. I had to just accept that God removed himself to teach me a valuable lesson.

Chapter 9

SPIRITUAL WARFARE
Ephesians 6:12

For our struggle is not against flesh and blood, but against the rulers, against the authorities, against the powers of this dark world and against the spiritual forces of evil in the heavenly realms

CHAPTER 10

This enemy who was out to distract and harm my path was only for me to see and no one else. I was battling a serpent undercover. On the flipside of things I was thankful because it made me stronger and wiser each day. I had to realize what I see and feel is between me and God.

I allowed divination to come in and take complete control over my life and in the end it was all a lie. Nothing was satisfying me. New Age practices made me feel more depressed than I already was and my soul felt so empty. Every void that I tried to fulfill was only temporary.

Witch doctors have a way of sticking to the same situation of reminding you about the miserable state that you were once in. I could simply be having a good day and my advisor would send me a message about the depressed state I was in prior to my healing state.

It takes you back to the place you're aiming to move away from. It's like a mixture of healing and manipulation. Some advisors are genuine in their profession but there are some that have a way of healing but also manipulating the situation to milk you out of more money.

Thinking back it was such a slap in the face to God. God has the answer to all things and at that phase in my life my total trust was in divination.

Witch doctors were aligning my path with the stars and another funny thing about it was there were no conversations related to God. It's pretty much a self-absorbed façade that the enemy has manipulated them into thinking that this is the way you should be living your life.

Walking through this spiritual realm I was introduced to the twin flame journey. I had a three year twin flame connection with three high profile women. Twin flames are mirror souls and are the rapid development of a deep connection and the sense that the relationship was meant to be. Rachel was my first flame and when that connection ended I met Trese who is a big time officer in Arkansas.

We met on social media through a mutual friend and as we got to know one another a little bit more I noticed her and Rachel had the same traits and similar backgrounds to the point of scaring me. The similarity was unreal. They even had the same body structure.

Our relationship lasted about six months. Once this connection ended I could feel a shift in my spirit. Another flame was about to appear but I had the feeling of conviction all over me and I was so disgusted with myself.

I had this open wound to the heart that kept attracting the same things. Twin flame journeys are life lessons. It's this detour that you have going in circles instead of God's way which is straight and narrow. My life all around was deceptive.

My spiritual, emotional, mental and physical life were all lies. Every dark force that I had allowed to come into my life had overtaken me and it just wasn't worth it in the end. I was more than ready to surrender my life to Christ.

ON A MISSION 2 TRANSITION

Chapter 10

DECEPTION

Colossians 3:9-10

Do not lie to each other, since you have taken off your old self with it's practices and have put on the new self, which is being renewed in knowledge in the image of it's Creator

CHAPTER 11

One day after waking up and realizing all of the things that I allowed to come in and take me off my true path, I decided to let go of everything, literally that was not of God. I felt overall with anything that's of negativity I no longer wanted to partake in.

I didn't think everything that I allowed in my life that was not of God was in vain, I felt with all of the things that I allowed and went through since childhood can help someone through my story.

One morning getting out of bed I walked in the bathroom and dumped my sage, crystals, tarot cards account and my online connections with spiritual advisors. I felt in order for me to hear God I had to wipe out everything and repent to start fresh.

In the beginning I felt that letting go of everything that was not of God would be some type of force but surprisingly it happened naturally for me. Going through so much in every aspect of my life with the things I was giving up, I knew deep within it couldn't give me the love and support of Christ.

After my breakthrough I began to see a new beginning with my family as well. It gave me this feeling towards my husband and son that I've never had before. It allowed me to see what life really should be and to appreciate what's right in front of me everyday.

Partaking in so much rebellion God could have easily taken me out and I'm so thankful for His grace and mercy. I thank Him for allowing me to go through all of this and getting myself out of the way and allowing His work to continually build my faith.

When you are sincere about changing your life for the better, God will move in your life and the old will pass away. Years back I would pray when I was going through something and once I got well I would go back to those same habits but this time around was different. I knew sincerely I was delivered.

I feel if I was to go back to my old habits I would die or get into something a lot deeper to the point of no return. God is definitely not to be played and tampered with. For me to still be alive it just makes me love the Most High so much more. I take Christ with me every step of the way.

My breakthrough was at the age of 42. This particular number will always remain special to me. Just to sit back and look at all of the things God brought me out of and to tell my story along with living a righteous life. The storm wasn't definitely by accident. God was building my confidence and He's instilling so much within me to the point of handling every situation I encounter. I am free indeed.

Chapter 11

BREAKTHROUGH

Isaiah 43:19

Behold, I am doing a new thing; now it springs forth, do you not perceive it? I will make a way in the wilderness and rivers in the desert

CHAPTER 12

I'm so thankful for God saving me, not because of righteous things I've done, but because of His mercy. He saved me through the washing of rebirth and renewal by the Holy Spirit. (Titus 3:5) He knows the plans He has in mind for me and they are plans for peace, not disaster, to give me a future filled with hope. (Jeremiah 29:11)

He reveals the deep things of darkness and brings deep shadows into the light. (Job 12:22) His flesh is my true food, and his blood is my true drink. His flesh abides in me, and I in Him. (John 6:55-56) I listen to Him daily and dwell in safety, He secures me from the fear of evil. (Proverbs 1:33)

He set up a kingdom through me to give him glory and it shall never be destroyed and it shall stand forever. (Daniel 2:44) He taught me to make a tree good so that its fruit will be good or make a tree bad and its fruits will be bad, for a tree is recognized by its fruit. (Matthew 12:33)

I walk in all His ways that He has commanded me to, so that I may live and prosper and prolong my days in the land that I will possess. (Deuteronomy 5:33) The Lord is gracious and full of compassion; slow to anger, and of great mercy. The Lord is good to all: And His tender mercies are over all His works. (Psalms 145:8-9)

I humble myself under His mighty hand so that at the proper time He may exalt me, casting all my anxieties on Him, because He cares for me. (1 Peter 5:6-7)

Trust in the Lord with all your heart and lean not on your own understanding. In all your ways submit to Him, and He will make your paths straight. (Proverbs 3:5-6)

For God so loved the world that He gave His only begotten son that whoever believes in Him should not perish but have eternal life. (John 3:16)

Do not be anxious about anything but in every situation by prayer and petition, with thanksgiving, present your request to God. And the peace of God, which transcends all understanding, will guard your hearts and your minds in Christ Jesus. (Philippians 4:6-7)

He's exalted, then, to the right hand of God, He has received from the Father the promised Holy Spirit and has poured out what I now see and hear. (Acts 2:33) When you pray, don't worry about how God will do it. Just trust that He has control of it all.

Final Chapter

REBIRTH
Titus 3:5

He saved us, not because of righteous things we had done, but because of his mercy. He saved us through the washing of rebirth and renewal by the Holy Spirit